Mother Knows Best

The NEW Story of Notre Dame

MOTHER KNOWS BEST

The NEW Story of Notre Dame

ATTY. WILLIAM O'CONNOR

To order additional copies of this book, contact:
Xlibris Corporation
1-888-795-4274
www.Xlibris.com
Orders@Xlibris.com
113055

TABLE OF CONTENTS

To the principles that endure through
the people who live them.

I am fortunate to know many.

William Joseph O'Connor

FOREWORD

Don't be fooled. This book may not look large, but find a spare hour and you will think otherwise. It contains no footnotes, research, bibliography, or other useless stuff. I never read them anyway. Bet you don't either. You will also find that our characters are very special to us, and will be to you when you learn of them. It will be like they are speaking to you. They did to me.

William Joseph O'Connor

DISCLAIMER

Now for the obligatory disclaimer. The views expressed in this book are not the views of the University of Notre Dame, or her officials. They are exclusively the views of the author, William Joseph O'Connor, and they just happen to be the correct ones, and are subject to the protection of the copyright laws of the United States.

CHAPTER ONE
THERE'S MORE AT THE DORM

Whether Zahm, Stanford, Dillon, Lyons, or Badin, there always was more in dorm life at Notre Dame, like a blaring rock opera, trying to find your dorm after a late night party, or studying for your weekly Emil T. Quiz while the jerk next door kept blaring the same rock opera. Irish dorms were living Claddagh rings, where friendship, loyalty, and love combined for lasting unity.

Dorm life started slowly when I met my two roommates in the command module of Apollo 13, called 232 Zahm, when my Dad recommended a haircut for one of them. Bad start Dad, real bad. No one's in ROTC yet, and can't you hear Joe Cocker next door? I spent freshman year with John Gilogly from Providence and Jim Kempa from Alsip. We got along well except when I acted like a teenage dope, usually when Jim studied for an Emil T. Quiz. That Emil T. never made me nervous. I showed him. I skipped his course for Rocks and Stars - Geology and Astrology, one of the three reasons I graduated. Space Tech and Sex & Marriage are the other two reasons.

Rocks and Stars was a very large class. I mean the students were very large. Tall too. Mostly football and basketball players, but don't get carried away now. There were no jock courses at Notre Dame then, now or ever. I mean, it's tough remembering that coal is black, the world is round, and the earth has only one moon. Father Shilts was a great guy, he taught us planets and the hardest course of all: eligibility.

In academics, I had my Dad eating out of my hand. For four years, he begged, he literally begged me to bring home a 3.0 for a semester. Could have done it any time, but I wanted to get even with him for sending me to a town without pity, a school without women. I pulled it off our last semester, senior year, and measured it off just right. Right on the nose - the coveted 3.0. Couldn't have done it without Space Technology. Space Tech got me a solid "A", just like five hundred seventeen other guys. What a professor! During tests, if you asked him a question about a question, he didn't give you guidance, he gave you the answer. He would literally give you the answer!! No matter how many times you asked!! Give that guy The Laetare Medal. Make him Secretary of Education. Wherever his is, he remains deeply, deeply loved. How did they keep this from Hesburgh?

Of course, Father Ted brought us co-education in '73. Of course, that meant no more male valedictorians, salutatorians, or top twenty-five finishes. Right from the get-go, Marianne O'Connor made valedictorian, so I sent home the Observer headline: "O'CONNOR NAMED VALEDICTORIAN". It was not well received.

Sex and Marriage satisfied religion requirements, and a whole lot more. It was rumored to be a skin flick surrounded by a few lectures, so no one missed the cinematic segments of class. Of course, it was immensely popular because we were all virgins and remained so until marriage. If you haven't noticed, this book is non-fiction with some elements of elasticity.

For every action, there is a reaction. For every Geology and Astrology, Space Tech, and Sex & Marriage, there was Calculus, Biology, and Statistics. Calculus: the first and final frontier. My first class ever. Almost my last. The administration building was not in good shape in 1970. On the fourth floor, we sat on the south side of the classroom so we wouldn't slide through the northern wall. Then in walks this guy in short sleeves and a pocket protector, and without a single word writes Professor Henry Peebles on the blackboard, and launches into full metal calculus lecture. It may as well have been in Chinese, dominated by an overriding thought: "Mom, can I come home now?". Professors Peebles and Van Meter combined their classes for the mid-term. My score was 43, a solid "B" on the curve. Then came second semester, and thank God for Finite Math and Professor Walter Langford, a class act and one of the first leaders of the Peace Corps.

Like I said, our room was smaller than the Apollo 13 command module, so we sought other places for space and concentration, like the hall basement and TV lounge, where the Cubs and Bulls would crash and burn in the wake of Knicks' and Mets' World championships, when I learned the meaning of "Ya Gotta Believe". Thanks Tug, I still do.

Most of the guys were from Boston, or farther east. I could tell because they talked funny, and they thought I did, too. Al Danza from Brooklyn, P.J. Bottari from Long Island, Steve

Merkle from Paramis and Dino Don Kennedy from "The City", (that's New York City for you Hoosiers). Dino had a uniform greeting: "Got a cigarette?", even if he had a full pack, even if you didn't smoke. He was Zahm's sport oracle, the sports columnist for the "Observer" who won everything, and hated to lose when he didn't, like our ping-pong match.

When defeat was inevitable, Dino kept muttering: "I hate to lose, I hate to lose." He really meant that he hated to lose to a seventeen year old Hoosier freshman. We had traces of that eastern stuffiness and midwestern defiance. So I made amends, gave him a cigarette, and told him the Cubs choked. Donnie and all the guys in Zahm were great guys. We were a Claddagh ring, still are.

Jim, John, and I met with instant social success. Three blind dates for the Barnum and Bailey circus. We made that long western walk to LeMans, determined to be John, Joe, and Jimmy instead of Moe, Larry, and Curly. I loved the circus, at least until I was eight years old, when the elephants were older than the clown jokes. But this visit revived the old appeal: "Wow, what an outfit on that girl on the trapeze. She must have sprayed it on". I suppressed those thoughts and remained a gentleman, for we escorted three very nice young women, probably as scared as we were, except no one was as scared as we were. Why does the walk from LeMans always seem longer than the walk to LeMans?

During our tenure, dorm rules were not strictly enforced, because there weren't any. Notre Dame closed early in the

Spring of '70 due to the Kent State incident, so there was a prolonged deferral of dorm discipline. So it was beer by the quart, case, keg, or truckload and even smoking pot was tolerated, not by me of course. Of course, this book is nonfiction with some elements of elasticity. Selling it was discouraged, like in early September of 1970 when my parents read their Chicago Tribune and its front page story of a drug bust in Zahm, on my floor, near my room.

Things worsened the following weekend, when Mom and Dad came for the home opener. While Mom visited the girls' room, Dad headed for my room, but forgot the exact location and entered the wrong room. Man oh man, was it ever the wrong room, when he barged in on a Zahm junior and a co-ed in the midst of the over and under, and I don't mean a Super Bowl bet. Had to forget the game for dad's electroshock. Aren't parietals a specie of flower?

There were a few surprises freshman year, none as great as the last, and no matter how many times I asked, my dad would never tell me the number of that wrong room. All great guys then and now, even without contact for years. A lasting Claddagh ring. And the girls? Is the circus in town?

CHAPTER TWO
TO SIR ABOVE

I. Ed Cronin, Ed Cronin, I sure was groanin',
        when I had Cronin
    His teaching style was quite direct, so some
        knowledge he would reflect
    Ed taught Novel, Speech, and English Lit,
        and in all three I was unfit
    He'd pound it in with sledge and hammer,
        yet still I failed prose and grammar.

II. My finest work, Ed turned to mud, so much
        red it looked like blood
    My papers Ed would so attack, they came
        back with more red than black
    O'Connor, son Ed would opine, "You've
        got to get your brain in line"
    You and I will meet a lot, and then we'll
        find out what you've got.

III. Then to Confession I was assigned, I'd rather
        have been jailed and fined.
    Ed's office in the 'brary's depths, three
        times a week to it I schleped
    Ed said, "Son, take it from the top, and
        through English you'll skip and hop"
    And with Ed's help, I soon got better, I
        even could write half a letter.

IV. Sometimes in class Ed would digress, so our
     learning was more, not less
   He'd speak of Emmet, and speak with glee,
     of when all Ireland is free
   Ed spoke of him with such great rapture,
     and of his speech to all his captors
   A speech of such grand elocution, made
     right before his execution.

Gone, our Ed will never be, a lasting presence, no memory.

I haven't seen Ed Cronin since he shook my hand at '74's commencement, but he's been present nonetheless. Don't be mistaken, it's Ed writing this chapter, he just let's me move the pen. Ed Cronin was no mere professor, he was a teacher - a teacher, a teacher who could pull authors from the average, a teacher who always taught for those of least ability, giving them the most ability. I was too dense to know it then, but every returned paper bore Ed's affection, every correction came from concern. That commitment culminated in a single event, the foremost achievement in the history of academics.

The Great Books Seminar was the heart and soul of the General Program, and the final exam was very final. The only test of the semester, a half hour oral exam hosted by your professor and a guest. Now that it's thirty-five years after graduation, I'll admit that I didn't quite get to all of the books for this seminar, maybe half. So two days before the ordeal, I trekked to the library with a few books and a pile of Cliff Notes. No, I did not need directions.

At eight forty-five a.m. I opened the classic Irish novel, "Tristan and Isolde". Twenty minutes later I thought: "Hey, this is pretty good.". Seven hours later, I thought: "Hey, that was real good.". A quick look at my Cliff Notes and I was ready to take my chances. For these tests, I was more frightened than walking to the Circle or LeMans. Then I entered the office and saw the guest professor, and choked on my kidneys: "Oh no, Oh no! Not Ed Cronin. God, not Ed Cronin! This isn't confession, this is Last Rites! He's gonna cut me up and have me served at the north dining hall. Oh well, at least I'll taste better than the pork tenderloin.". I quickly pondered the obvious delay tactics: "Professor, may I use the men's room and pound a few cyanide pills?". But like Kinnison lamented, I lacked the decency to follow through.

Than Ed led with: "Joe, let's talk a little about 'Tristan and Isolde'". A Stay of Execution, and for five minutes I'm an Irish oracle. Then Ed paused, and I'm waiting for: "Joe, let's talk about another book", or "Professor, is there another book you would like to discuss?" Instead, Ed said, "Joe, I have some more questions about Tristan and Isolde'". The Jackpot, the Lottery, a date with Terri Buck. For the next twenty-five minutes, Ed and I were like Hope and Crosby, Martin and Lewis, Holtz and the Option. I knew everything, Ed knew that I knew everything, and soon I knew that Ed knew that I knew everything. Ed wouldn't let me ace that test, he was going to do it for me.

Our dialogue was like Dean Smith's Four Corners' offense, holding the academic ball the entire half hour. Got 'em all right, every last one, even the last one: "Joe, was there more than one Isolde?". "Yes, Professor. There was Isolde of the White hand and Isolde of Ireland". Ed replied, "And who did Tristan marry?" Genius Boy: "Isolde of Ireland, of course", with a big, fat inflection on of course.

Ed and I, like Gondorf and Hooker, have kept this con for thirty-five years. Now it's out, and all of you have learned from Ed Cronin, the greatest teacher in the history of education, because the courses he taught were less important than the people he taught.

May I love others as much as Ed Cronin loved me.

CHAPTER THREE
THE QUIET MAN

DA-DA, DA-DA, DA-DA, DA-DA- DA-DA,
DA-DA, DA-DA, DA-DA, DA-DA-DA-DA,
DA-DA, DA-DA, DA-DA, DA!
DA-DA-DA-DA-DA-DA-DA-DA, DA, DA-DA

There, that should get you in a Quiet Man mood. If you need more, there is a Mapquest to Corby's on page eighty-seven. You guys know the definition of a great referee - you hardly know they're there. For forty-four years Dennis Stark was so effective we hardly knew he was there. While others amassed hours of community service, the Coach volunteered for years. He was special years before the Special Olympics, because his son Kenny is special.

In 1958 he created the Notre Dame Swimming program from a few drops of water, and coached it for the next twenty-five years. He coached swimming, he coached diving, he carried towels and cleaned the Rock all day, every day, after a full schedule of classes. A Quiet Man, he didn't need to raise his voice to instill or communicate discipline. For road trips, we left the circle at seven, and for a two meet trip, the new team stud arrived late, and we were gone. Defeat came twice without him, but discipline and authority were never an issue.

On February 23, 1974 we traveled to Illinois State - last meet of the year, last chance for our coach's one hundredth victory. Looked like this would be decided by a single point, and guess what? That was the margin, and in the last event we trailed by six points for three hundred ninety-nine yards, but not the last.

It was a coaching masterpiece, everyone contributed. Without a point from Pat Laughlin in the 50 Free, we lose. Without a point from Ed Graham in the 200 Back, we lose. Without victory from Bob Ebel in the three meter diving, who failed to place in the one meter, we lose. Like every last man, Bob came through and though our relay trailed in the third leg, I knew I just had to get us in range for our anchor, Jim "Virgil" Kane, and that usually meant within eyesight.

Victory by a point. Victory and our bench was bedlam, except our coach who still was the Quiet Man, at least until the post-game meal when some seniors ordered a bottle of champagne for him. The only cork that popped was coach's, who lost it the only time in memory, and a few seniors nearly lost their monograms.

Ed Cronin and The Quiet Man must have been related, for he too cared less for what he taught than the people he taught. That is why I speak for our team, every one of us, teammates forever.

May we care for others as much as our coach cared for us.

CHAPTER FOUR
MISTER ED

No, no talking horse in this book. For the most intriguing Ed ever at Notre Dame was "Fat Eddie", the towel man at the ROCK. They say first impressions are lasting, so after a fleeting glance, followed by: "You're looking good today, kid" I was certain I had made my last visit to the Rock. Of course, it was all innocent, just a different sort of introduction by a very nice person, a legend of Notre Dame.

Junior year, Coach Stark started a weekly "Goldbrick" award given to the guy who dogged it the most during the week's practice. Eddie presented the award every week along with a big, fat hug. Loafing in practice declined sharply, and Ed's legend spread over campus, especially the annual contest of Fat Eddie banners during football season. The hands down winner was on the south wall of Lyons proclaiming: "Fat Eddie says _____ them off the field". That one didn't have a lot of longevity with campus authorities, prude problems, you know.

Our Notre Dame was unique because of all its people, from Trustees to towel men. I would have received less of an education without Eddie, much less. Others too. Now he'll hand you a towel right after you give your spare change to the altruist.

May I love others as much as Eddie hoped to love me.

CHAPTER FIVE
WHEN YOU'RE ALONE AND LIFE IS MAKING YOU LONELY, YOU CAN ALWAYS GO - **DOWNTOWN!**

The math was harsh but simple. An all male university of six thousand next to a college of twelve hundred. So on weekends, thoughts turned to town, from Corby's to Kubiak's, and from Notre Dame to Niles. For the truly desperate, a condition that I quickly eclipsed, it was time to reach for a rendevous at "The Circle", hitchhiking for a car full of companionship, the ultimate test of luck. Not much hope for a kid voted "Most Quiet" in his class.

But wait, a teammate to the rescue. A man of circle-land, shrewd and experienced with South Bend socialites. A man who felt so sorry for me that he took me in, just like Luke and Yoda. Lesson number one, geography was critical, no hangin' with the crowd at The Circle. On campus, I would visit all the hallowed grounds - the Grotto, Sacred Heart, and the revered Chris Mecca cut-off, one block east of the circle, where the Circle King could work his magic without interference.

For circle success, you had to learn to deal with failure, but after six or seven bust outs, E-harmony. Two girls invited us into their car, and if Chris swam the butterfly as fast as he evaporated into the back seat, Mark Spitz would be short one medal. But then again, Spitz never won gold at The Circle, did he?

We could tell they were nice girls since they were nice

enough to bring liquor. A couple slugs of sloe gin and I started to fizz. "To Flanner with the speed of lighting", exhorted the king. "There's a party on my floor". What a party it was. Wall to wall people, ear-splitting Sly, garbage can Wapatulla, and I had date, I had a date. For chrissake, I had a date. What the hell do I do now? Fortunately, my date cooperated as she was affectionate and a little fizzed herself.

Then the king approached and in the ultimate act of benevolence said, "Hey Joey-O, if you would like to be alone with your friend, you can use my room". Love like this, no Circle king has. Sorry, no sordid and steamy encounter here, I'll stick to non-fiction, and let others lapse into fictional amorous avalanche.

For underclassmen, the forcefield of legal eighteen year old drinking in Michigan was overpowering. From the concrete floor at Jay's to the dance floor at Kubiak's, there was a certain comfort in legality, even in the lounge at Shula's. I broke as many schooners on Jay's floor as feet I stepped on at Kubiak's doing the Pennsylvania Polka. Met a great guy named Frank. Just Frank, the most non-pretentious pretension candidate ever. Couldn't be a lawyer now.

Of course, besides going into town, we brought the town to us. For Mardi Gras, for An Tostal, and other events, Barat, Mundelein, and other schools would send students by the bus loads. This wasn't well received in some circles, when two older college students wrote the Observer claiming that the practice was: "Disgusting, like bringing in meat on the hoof".

Of course, Notre Dame Nation rushed to the defense of its guests, in this shootout at the N.D. Corral, as the opening shot prompted the largest editorial response in Observer history including:

"When local supply is sparse and of inferior quality, we are forced to import" - signed the Cattlemens Association.

It looks like these were letters better off not written, but sticks and stones is always a good yardstick, and we were only teenagers.

Another off-campus treat was the Armory parties, with more beer throwing than beer drinking, to a loud, loud, rock band. Soaked with Strohs' by the second set, and there's nothing like a Budweiser hug. Let's do it again, and hope my date doesn't leave with the drummer, again.

May I love others the way I hoped girls from town would love me.

CHAPTER SIX
KICKIN' AND A GOUGIN' IN THE MUD
AND THE BLOOD AND THE BEER

I may be speaking heresy, but "Knute Rockne, All-American" has competition for greatest football movie of all time, thanks to Eddie Albert, Bernadette Peters, Richard Kiel, and Burt Reynolds in 1974's "The Longest Yard". The opening scene alone was Oscar worthy, when Burt's live-in girlfriend tries to stab him and he responds: "I think the love has gone out of our relationship". He proceeds to steal her Bentley and dumps it into a canal, then calls the arresting officers "Mutt" and "Jeff".

Oscars all for screen play, actor, and especially Bernadette's beehive, when Burt asks her: "I love your hair, do you get spiders in it?". The football violence was also exceptional. The quote: "I think I broke his f-ing neck" after a clothesline, and the same for same thing bullets thrown at the groin of Ray Nitscke.

But that was only a movie. For real football lovers, the real contact came a kickin' and a gougin' in the mud, and the blood, and the beer known as Inter-hall football. Kickin' and a gougin' in the mud, no pristine fields for them, they would have played on 31. Kickin' and a gougin' in the blood, since their equipment was from the 70's - the 1870's. Kickin' and a gougin' in the beer, as beer was in them from a fortnight, or sooner.

They played without scholarships or compulsion, they

played for the love of the game. They played with emotion, they played with execution, and sometimes they played with anger, as some hall rivalries, for intensity purposes, were a shade short of S.C.

One such rivalry was Zahm - Holy Cross, the grizzled veterans versus the talented and occasionally brazen upstarts. I lived with two of Zahm's grizzled veterans, Jack Leicht and Kerry Powers, like me, far more veteran now. It seemed like their joints creaked louder than the doors on Jack's ancient Chevy Nova. The showdown with Holy Cross went well into the playoffs, and at night on the artificial turf at Cartier. Two things stand out in that game, the magnificently dirty play of Zahm's Joe Greff at cornerback, and the play that changed the game.

An early Zahm out pattern was picked off at the Holy Cross goal line, and it looked like a clear hundred yard dash to score. But even though the Zahm's Phil "The Rock" Weckworth was on the opposite side of the field, he raced one hundred twenty yards to stop it. After that, Zahm could not be stopped, just like when Penick ran for seventy-six in seventy- three

Like every football team Zahm, Holy Cross, and all our hall teams shared a special bond. Special because they left their blood on the field, and sprained ankles, torn ligaments, separated shoulders, concussions, and their strange commitment to play with and after them. That's why players come and go, but teammates last forever, an allegiance obvious even to non-combatants.

CHAPTER SEVEN
THE MARX OF ZORRO

Out of the night, when the full moon is bight, rides the horseman known as Zorro. Zorro, Zorro!, the fox so cunning and free. Zorro, Zorro!, who makes the sign of the "Z".

When I was a very young boy, our family lived in a beautiful little bungalow on the south side of Hammond. I drive past every opportunity, because I know miracles happen there. Like on Sunday nights during the fall and winter months, when my brothers and I would gather in front of the television with our Dad at six o'clock to watch Zorro, The Swamp Fox, Davey Crockett, or Johnny Tremaine and The Sons of Liberty. Relax now, relax. The Sons of Liberty were not at O'Bama's last town hall meeting, and only priests are real end of life counselors.

After Disney, it was popcorn, root beer, and Bonanza. For Dad, it was beer and Bonanaza, soldiers saved from a Stroh's six pack stretched from Friday until Sunday. Seems like a lifetime ago, but needs no further description other than the feet in our pajamas, just like yours. I'm alone in front of the television now, but we'll be together soon to watch Guy Williams zip another "Z" on the lower abdomen of Sargent Garcia. Sarge sure hopes Guy made this week's fencing lesson. Now back to non-fiction.

Make no mistake, and when I begin with 'Make no mistake', I'm here to tell you of one tough hombre. Greg Marx never played left defensive tackle for Notre Dame, he never played at all. When 245 was big, Greg was 275 and quicker than Hesburgh's brain. Greg ate offensive linemen and spit them into the backfield like so many sunflower seeds, and surged to quarterbacks faster than his son's F-14. He gave no quarter and never took a cheap shot, except when he could get away with it.

Like SC '70, when Patulski was speared on a punt return. Benches cleared but Greg needed no help as he swung his helmet at circled Trojans like a horizontal circular saw. The boys from Redondo Beach could only stand clear and marvel at the rage.

SC '86 was the next time I saw Greg in competition. This time up close and personal, as we witnessed one of those stupid post-game confrontations, when a tipsy young Trojan sucker punched a mildly inebriated, (and I'm being charitable here), old Irishman. Blood Alley in an instant, and five Trojans were a band on the run. But they could not outrun rage, and took refuge in a bus full of friends. Undeterred, Greg stood on the front bumper and pounded the windshield 'til it nearly shattered. Since the bus driver had a close up view of the face of rage, he wisely relented and opened the door. Greg went in alone. Of course, I would have entered too, but I had to secure the perimeter. Moments later, Greg emerged with the culprit, and handed him over to county police. Then we headed home, into a Hammond sunset.

I always hoped to stand a hero; I was fortunate to stand with one.

CHAPTER EIGHT
THE HEAVE ON THE EVE

Creedence Clearwater Revival couldn't stop the rain since they hadn't recorded the song yet, so most of the 59,075 fans at the 1970 Purdue massacre shouted for Ara to stop it when Larry Parker cruised fifty-five untouched yards down the near sideline on his first Irish touch.

The previous evening, six thousand young men drown in a sea of dirt, sweat, and tears in the old field house, Rocky Bleier's first stop after the VA and Vietnam. Even before he spoke it was an emotional scene, for it was obvious the icon was in more than mild discomfort. References to God, Country, and Notre Dame were not cliches then nor now, and were delivered to a sea of emotional wrecks. Proud of it too.

Then Ara. Even his approach incited frenzy, as his black eyes could pierce the library's granite Christ as well as transgressions in practice. Like many coaches, he was kinder in public, often stern to his sons, every player his own, just like his own, who got it worse than the rest. Of course, all who competed have received the wrath of leadership from some great man or woman, leaders looked to long after competition, who set impossible goals, drove us relentlessly to reach them, and upon achievement remarked: "Good job, I think you can do more".

Whether grade school, high school, or college, they coach us more now than ever. Like most, my first coach was dad. Would have been an outstanding college athlete except for the intervention of the Japanese Imperial Army, and like yours, he tutored everything from football to baseball to ping-pong, and he's still upset over my first victory. As young boys, we didn't love them, we revered them, and still do. That's how it was with Ara, unsurpassed campus wide in handball, golf, and respect, the Pa Cartwright of six thousand sons on Our Lady's Ponderosa.

Young people, boys for certain, look to a coach, parent, a teacher, or other mentor for inspiration and spark. When they do, they grab on and never let go. Young people need that, and if you hadn't noticed, us old people do too. Coaches are naturals for this, and coaches like Ara, Coach Lou, The Quiet Man, and others possess unnatural spark-generating ability. We were fortunate to find them.

Most were unaware that Ara was a playwright until later in his career, when he debuted a one-night drama greater than "Othello", more exciting than "The Jersey Boys", and more controversial than a million Monologues. It debuted New Year's Eve '73 to 80,000 live, at a large, outdoor southern theater with millions more watching on television. Riveting from start to finish, with a finishing save in '73 from the Class of '74.

With our heroes backs to the end line, Ara called "The Heave on the Eve", which took two timeouts - one to tell the players, and one to revive them. Then two dropped ten and heaved it into the darkness for what seemed an eternity, until it reached the webs of Webber, safe then, safe now, safe forever, as some say he hasn't let go, the play that brought us victory, the play that brought a National Championship, and best of all, the play that left Bud cold. Howard wasn't too happy either. We all were there then, in person or not, just like now, because classmates come and go, teammates last forever, just like the Night Before New Year's:

Twas the Night before New Year's, and in South Louziana
The Irish arrived to defeat Alabama
Some Catholics were hung in the late afternoon
When they got too rowdy in a Cajun Saloon
When Conflict Began, the Fans seemed all Tide
Then Irish Appeared all on the Victory's Side
And then for a hundred Alfonse danced, dodged and juked
While up in the booth, Bud Wilkinson puked
And in every quarter, we all prayed to God
that Potempa'd get in there and kill Richard Todd
Who threw to a receiver, who then threw it back,
and it seemed so unfair in the score we did lack
But the Irish undaunted marched back down the field
But the Crimson Tide defense would not totally yield
Then the Judge came through, but needed some luck
He got us three points, though his kick really sucked
Now that kick is known near and afar
As that wonderful time when the Judge passed the Bar
Then 'Bama came back, but stopped at midfield
Red kicked to our one, the game's fate unsealed
Not even God knew what was up Ara's sleeve
For it was His Mother who called the last heave
Then on all shoulders our Ara did ride
He could not stop the rain, but he did stem the Tide

Ara was ever busy, but always found time for friends and strangers alike, and even found time to send a note for a brother's eulogy. Since then, Mark stands outside Heaven's gate and he's not moving until Ara arrives. He's been joined by three nice kids from down Tucson Way, so nice we sing of them:

<u>Tucson Way</u>

There lives a lovely girl down Tucson way,
becoming more beautiful day by day,
She loves her brothers and sister so,
together, a family forever more.
This pretty young girl has lots of friends,
with love and caring that never ends,
Their bond is always and always lives,
for giving always then always give.
Family, is who we are, friendship, our biggest part,
Teamwork, to reach our goals,
binding together our hearts and souls.
To give to others is the best kind,
for giving more is the way they find,
Their inspiration comes from above,
and all together, its' known as love.
Family, is who we are, friendship, our biggest part,
Teamwork - to reach our goals, binding
together our hearts and souls,
So think of them each and every day,
Especially pretty Marcia down Tucson Way,
Tucson Way...Pretty Marcia...Tucson Way.

May we all have the courage found down Tucson Way.

CHAPTER NINE
A SHOT AND A BEAR

One southern Bear down, but some undefeated Western bruins will arrive in three weeks after eighty-eight consecutive meals. How do you plan for perfection? Only Digger knew, like cutting down the nets after Friday's practice, and cutting off Big Red from the ball the next afternoon, thanks to the muscle, elbows, and rear end of John Shumate.

The Irish only led once, thanks to A.D.'s leveling some sequoias, and even loyalists couldn't believe Ice iced it until Enberg's: "Walton...Meyers...Shumate... it's over!!". Seventy-One for seventy-four , seventy for the Redondo Beach crowd, and for a moment, the legend with the rolled up program returned to mortality, bested by uniforms only a mother could love, and the bell-bottomed suit of their coach.

May we all be as courageous as Digger's wardrobe.

CHAPTER TEN
LOGAN'S RUN AND THE "Y" GUYS

"Logan's Run" was an above average '72 sci-fi flick starring Michael York in a futuristic society, where no one got too futuristic because the government killed everyone at the age of thirty. Logan and his girlfriend ran, and ran, and ran. Ultimately they survived. Kind of disappointing, really. Some times life tends to breed skepticism, doesn't it?

Of course, this flick was fiction, and the real Logan's Run was every Thursday afternoon to Logan Center, formerly known as Logan Center for the R-word. Thank God they got rid of the R-word, there and just about everywhere. At our first freshman meeting, The Quiet Man suggested we volunteer there. Then an upperclassman advised I spend some time there if I wanted to have a snowball's chance of making the traveling team.

So most Thursdays, Ed Strack, Ed Graham, John Cleaver, Doug Free, Chris Mecca and I lugged it over to Logan. But those were only our real names, for when we arrived, we became Eddie, Eddie, Johnny, Douggie, Chrissy, and Joey, because the guys we worked with were Tommy, Billy, Johnny, and a bunch of other guys whose names ended in y. The "Y" guys. What a wonderful Claddagh Ring we were, every unified Thursday, and every other day for that matter.

There was a short period of adjustment for us college guys with the Y guys, especially for this green, seventeen year old Hoosier kid. When it came to dressing, undressing, swimming instructions, and all the other stuff there were no problems, except sometimes the guys had difficulty with basic mathematics, like the numbers one and two. Small thing then, fond memory now, just the need for a little extra Claddagh care. Come to think of it, I needed that type of assistance myself after a few future frolics.

We gave them swim instruction, we played water basketball, and even taught them that there are five "Wubs" in Wub-Wub-Wub-Wub-Wub. Did we teach them a lot? Did they learn a lot? Probably not much, and that really didn't matter at all. Because for an hour a week, they had fun, I really mean we had fun. We laughed, we high-fived, we splashed them a little, they splashed us a lot, and there was bedlam when a Y-guy nailed a baseline jumper.

But it was really Eddie, Eddie, Johnny, Douggie, Chrissy, and Joey who were slow on the uptake. We realized only later that we were not teaching them, but they were teaching us. They taught us that they were not retarded, they taught us that they were not freaks, most of all they taught us they were just like us, except for a special challenge which made them a lot more special.

I quickly became Captain Renot: "I'm shocked, The Quiet Man's kid is in the pool". Kenny's impact, like all the Y-guys far exceeded immediate family scope, and he kept Bonnie Doons in the black for decades.

We all have our fondest campus moments, but they're all in competition for second place. At our reunion a year ago, eight hundred gathered in the South Dinning Hall, all set to welcome and honor The Quiet Man. But even quiet men can be sneaks sometimes, especially those who prefer the recognition of others to themselves, so before our coach was recognized, we heard:

"Before our Coach speaks, let me introduce the most important person in the history of our program, and I just know, that as he approaches the podium, it will cause you to stand, shout, clap, and raise a racket that will shake the foundation of this beautiful old building. It is a high honor and a profound privilege to present the finest man among us, the recipient of the University's Lifetime Achievement Award, Kenny Stark".

It was a very emotional scene as Kenny approached the podium with the assistance of his brother Craig. Kenny accepted the plaque acknowledging his performance, inspiration and leadership. The plaque was in the same shape, color, and contained the same language as the team's most coveted award, given by a bunch of rank sentimentalists.

By the way, don't tell anyone that we did not seek the University's authorization for the award. Acclamation was good enough for us, and if they want it back, they are going to have to get through eight hundred rank sentimentalists. I spoke to The Quiet Man a few months later, who advised that Kenny had shown his award to everyone, several times. Mission accomplished. Mission accomplished.

The Y-guys are older now, and they are James, Doug, Ron, and Steve. I guess they've gotten more formal with age. They live in a group home in Dyer, Indiana - Special then, special now, special always. Their home is managed by a special person. I know, I married her.

A final point, back to "Logan's Run", when government authorized death of the defenseless, without notice, without trial, without appeal or review, without mercy. Death by choice, death by the millions. These Hollywood types can dream up anything, can't they?

May we love others as much as the Y-guys loved life.

May we love those who had it taken.

CHAPTER ELEVEN
FOUR FOR FOUR

Ten chapters in, and I can feel a slight fade in my creative nirvana from the previous nine, so I'll make the turn with four short subjects.....

THE FOOD COURT

I've had extensive experience dining in the North and South dining halls. I should say that I have extensive experience eating at the North and South eating halls, where extra veal parmesans were left for Lefty Smith, and where mashed potatoes still cling to the sides of South Bend sewers. Of course, the food was pretty decent overall, I just couldn't resist the alliteration. Like many, I ate a million red Jell-O cubes. Not strawberry, not cherry, not raspberry. Just red, the don't ask - don't tell flavor. Just like red pop. Ya' know, maybe they were red pop, jellified.

Steak Night provided quarterly relief if you didn't get hurt during the Oklahoma Food Rush, and occasionally hall rivalries would boil over into food fights, and like the contact during inter-hall football, these fights were real, not the "Animal House" variety. We stay buried in our bunkers 'neath the dining tables, Spartan shields (food trays) raised high in defense. Effective ammunition was at a premium, often limited to those Jell-O cubes. Grab a handful, bite off two or three, like pulling out a grenade pin out with your teeth, then let fly. Jell-O and mashed potatoes never did much damage, so after a few volleys we were winging water glasses instead of Jell-O, at which point security would step in like referees breaking up a hockey fight.

Of course, there was a certain satisfaction in reviewing the post food fight scene, sort of like Patton reviewing a North African beach. With co-education, we had more manners, more couth, and no food fights. The sacrifices we made for progress.

Those without vehicles usually were limited to Rocco's, Louie's, the Library or a Nicky's Cheeseburger for off-campus culinary satisfaction. Their food was great, as were their carding practices:

WAITER: *"How old are you?*
*"*FRESHMAN: *"I'm twenty-one."*
WAITER: *"Bud or Old Style?"*

Like I said, the food was fantastic for the bizarre appetites of starving young men.

In those days I was 6' 2", one seventy-two, size twenty-eight Levis. Things change with time, barely get into a size thirty now. Curly and I made frequent trips to Louie's to down roast beef sandwiches while waiting for an extra large pizza. Our friend Johnny would down a bottle of Strawberry Hill, and when the pizza arrived, he'd down most of another. Now I think he's working as a sommelier. Of course, it always came back in the bushes between the Circle and La Forturne. For the late night gourmet, there was Nicky's Cheeseburger, anything to get "Band On The Run" played thirty consecutive times expunged from your system.

There was another fine dining hall tradition which ended mercifully with co-education, captaincy transfer in varsity sports. The incoming and outgoing captain shared a meal, without silverware. First done wins. Real messy the year spaghetti was featured.

A final note, our dining point of elegance, The Wooden Keg has been gone for some time, now there's a "Mr. Moo". Not the Keg, but it'll doo.

SENOR K

First year Spanish, first floor O'Shag, this guy just can't be the professor. He tells us his name, to a chain reaction of "huh?" Then he writes it on the board, to a chain reaction of "huh?", one of those unspellable Polish names - so unspellable, we doubted that even he spelled it correctly. He was soon "Senor K", and quickly became one of us: married, a kid, and a second year law student, soon to be the fate of some of us. Regular guy, too, we hoped that would be the fate of all of us.

A scheduling disaster arose, since Senor K's class was in the afternoon and conflicted with practice. Senor had the easy answer, "Just come to my 9:00 o'clock and I'm sure the Dean's Office will approve it". The Dean's Office didn't:

ASSISTANT DEAN (Senor Stuffiness): *"O'Connor, did you come to Notre Dame for an education or athletics?"*

O'CONNOR (after a lengthy pause & in his best Jack Bennyesque): *"I'm thinking it over!"*

Despite the official decision, I sort of unofficially attended the morning class the rest of the semester, and Senor K cooked the books. I told you he was a regular guy, maybe not so regular as Senor K and his spouse provided Notre Dame educations for all five of their children. Now there are a couple of tough hombres.

Senor K has practiced law in Lake County since '74, and I ran into him for the first time at a Bar Association function in 1980. Still concerned for his students, he asked if I retained a grasp of Spanish, if some of his teaching got through. I said to him, "Si". He said, "Still a smart-ass, aren't you?", and I answered, "Si".

I CAN'T WAIT TO GRADUATE

"The Graduate" may of been the best attended on-campus movie selection in the history of the University. It had profound and immediate impact. Hundreds wanted to date Katherine Ross, while hundreds more wanted to sleep with Anne Bancroft. You know, the old totally physical, no commitment thing. Of course, such relationships were purely fiction at Notre Dame.

Speaking of The Graduate - he taught freshman year English, a graduate assistant. In class he played "White Bird" - he played it, and played it, and played it, and played it:

White bird, in a Golden Cage, Alone
White Bird, in a Golden Cage, Alone
White Bird Must Fly, He Will Die
White Bird Must Fly, He Will Die
White Bird Must Fly, He Will Die - I - I - I, He Will Die - I - I - I
He Will Die I - I - I, I - I - I

The Graduate requested our evaluation. My first draft:

"Worst song written in the history of music, and
not just folk music, The lyrics were
totally without imagination,
and the guitar background could have
been played by a 5 year old
with eight broken fingers."

Then I realized The Graduate loved this song and the group. So I penned a revised draft, realizing that diplomacy often serves better than candor, a principle that has saved my marriage repeatedly. Revised draft:

"Undoubtedly the musical masterpiece of our time,
each line the product of compelling
genius, each part moving,
and of course the whole more compelling than the parts,
with a guitar background a literal
symphony of strings and fingers."

I did well in freshman year English.

CHAPTER TWELVE
KING OF A QUEEN'S CAMPUS

It was another dim and dingy spring semester in '73. The sky wore gray, we wore blue, until a late March Monday when someone shouted:

LOOK, ATOP BADIN HALL! IT'S A BIRD! IT'S A PLANE! IT'S A KING!!!"

As a cloud of smoke wafted westward, the king appeared and smiled as he peered down upon the bewildering panorama spread upon the green quadrangle below. But he was not the king. He was not a king, he was our king, cloned from all of us in a single warped experiment.

The King was introduced by All-American defensive end Walt Patulski, first pick in the NFL Draft, and more importantly, the one who saved me from being killed by Ralph Stepaniak when I elbowed him in the nose in a pick-up game at the Rock.

All-American tears flowed as the All-American related: "I was a 98 pound weakling until I met the King, I couldn't bench press a marshmallow, and I even got beat up by Southern Cal song girls". Walt pledged his life, his fealty, and his senior bar card, gratefully accepted by the King, a junior. Thereafter, Walt was no longer Walt but Sir Walter, Lord and Protector of the Campus, Sergeant at Arms of the campaign. Thousands followed suit. The King was one of us, a royal stud without royal blood, a plebeian destined for greatness.

What type of government was promised by our master? None really. He promised no policies, only power, an oligarchy, a term that even had geeks running for their dictionaries. While the King publicly advocated power vested in a few, he really meant himself. We accepted, and obeyed.

How better to defy authority than name a cat for running mate? When university officials insisted on a student ID, they got one. The Badin scientists immediately furnished feline identification for a feline more qualified than most of the student body.

Had the campaign been a prizefight, they would of have stopped it. Royal agents infiltrated the south dinning hall and blared "Pomp and Circumstance" on the sound system, then his highness made his royal entry, regaled in a flowing red cape and a cardboard Burger King crown. Then his highness was approached by a senior on crutches, but once the king touched his shoulder and gently said, "Walk my son", the former invalid not only walked, he won the hundred the next day at Bowling Green.

While non-believers think this event was staged, loyalists knew the game plan. Though unconventional, our king had a sense of history. Stealing the "V" for victory sign from Winston Churchill, The King combined it with the best of Chicago political tradition. "V" is for vote, two is for twice,

"VOTE TWICE". The double vote was unneeded as the king won eighty-five percent of the vote, a record by even Chicago standards.

The king ruled with distinction, although Miss America could have done without the cigar and bodyguards. In dramatic lore, he was known as "The King". In reality, he is The King. I told you we were loyal.

Thank you your highness, for making Spring of '73 far less dim and dingy, a light that shines today. The king now rules Fort Dodge, Iowa, a kingly doctor dispensing personal treatment and justice to his subjects. The whereabouts of the cat are currently unknown, a troubling development in the kingdom. He is a gray and black tabby who answers to the name "Uncandidate Cat" and he will be carrying a Notre Dame student ID.

May I love others as much as The King loved his subjects.

CHAPTER THIRTEEN
LITTLE BIG MAN MEETS GODZILLA

"You go down there gen'rl, those ain't women and children down there, them's Cheyenne braves. You go down there gen'rl, if you got the nerve." With those words, a lone muleskinner sent General Custer into the Little Big Horn.

Neither Lou Holtz nor his contributions were little, they were big, man. Another coach kinder in public than in practice, where he became Godzilla, snorting smoke, breathing fire, and stomping on miscues like the skyscrapers of Tokyo, when practices were closed not to protect game plans, but to prevent his arrest.

He paced the sidelines like an expectant father, waiting for his offense to deliver a score. His children came often, mostly by option. Lou and Notre Dame loved the option, but in football only, because when it comes to life, we never run the option. Lou loved Notre Dame, maybe did not long to leave, but has never said a discouraging word, whatever the range. His remains a presence in spirit, and even in song - "The Ballad of Lou Holtz" to the melody *I Know I'll Never Find Another You, The Seekers, 1964*:

There's a golf course somewhere, he
calls the Promised Land.
He's had lots of tee times, due to unhappy fans.
At one time he was a hero; But then they lost a few.
So they went out looking for some rope for Lou.

When you coach the Irish, you get a lot of help
From a million head coaches, who squeal, whine and yelp.
Because they all want perfection, so don't lose one or two
Or they'll go out looking for another Lou.
It's a long, long shadow that's cast down off that dome.
If you drop two or more you might go home, might go home!
He loves Bill and Mary, the Hogs and N.C. State;
And those Gophers and Gamecocks
they all have been just great.
But his first love is the Irish, to them he's always true.
And that's why we'll never find another Lou.
Yes, I know we'll never find another Lou.

CHAPTER FOURTEEN
FIST AND SHOUT

Da-Da, Da-Da-Da, Da-Da-Da, Da-Da-Da,
Da-Da, Da-Da-Da, Da-Da-Da, Da-Da-Da,
Da-Da-Da-Da, Da-Da-Da,
Da-Da-Da-Da-Da-Da-Da

Wasn't the original Rocky great? Couldn't expect much of five sequels, especially when the supporting actors were Mr. T, Tommy Morrison, and a robot. Besides, the star had expanded to *"Over, it's never over!!!"* (Rambo) and *"I'm your worst nightmare"*. (Cobra).

Of course, Rocky was to boxing as The Longest Yard was to football. So for real training, real boxing, and real blood it was the Bengal Bouts. The creation and tradition of Dominic Napolitano, another revered quiet man, more careful in matchmaking than Dr. Phil. When he told a young boxer: *"You're going to become a very dangerous person, you're gonna spit lighting and crap thunder"*, he really did spit lightning and crap thunder. Dorm life was tough at Bengal Bouts time.

One of Dominic's prize pupils was Pat McGrath, middleweight champion for four consecutive years, now a physician. Maybe we should call him the Fight Doctor, One of the Fighting McGraths, brothers, cousins, I think even a sister and grandmother, won Bengal Bouts titles. Cousin John, now a not-so-light heavyweight won future championships in character and loyalty.

In large part, Dominic was like the other great coaches at Notre Dame who taught first that you represented Notre Dame, then that you competed for her, then for your teammates, then against the opposition. Most of all, like all great coaches and teachers, he taught that you competed against yourself, and that the competition lasted long after the ball stopped bouncing. Fortunately, these lessons have been taught by Muffet McGraw and her colleagues despite their late arrival. While there were no women coaches until '73, they caught up fast, didn't they?

CHAPTER FIFTHTEEN
GO DOWN GAMBLIN'

Now let me impart some valuable lessons for generations to come: #1 - If you sit down at a card game and don't see any suckers, get the hell out of there because your it. #2 - Never play golf for money against someone who you've never seen play before.

I learned #2 the hard way. The hard way from a hall mate named Hans. Hans had that innocent milk and cookies look which masked irons by radar. Power versus precision, and precision won easily. Had me down to my speedo by the turn. Losing money hurt; losing face hurt more, but I sure learned my lesson.

Of course, we did not have a bookie in Zahm Hall. We called him an investment counselor. College football mostly, and nothing too heavy. Right. Now there's some real elasticity. We also had an occasional poker game, like every occasional Wednesday night. Wednesday night from 8 o'clock to 7 o'clock the next morning, grab breakfast at the north dining hall, cut class and sleep all day. Guess I know how I screwed up the LSAT. Twice.

Lesson Three. Never speak to family members about gambling of any nature. They're much better off and so are you. If you break Rule Number Three, then invoke Rule Number Four. Lie. Lie relentlessly. Lie without hesitation, as in:

"How'd it go, dear?"

"Oh, won a few hundred."

It won't help anyone if your spouse finds out that you blew two grand doubling down on sixteen, and then hit the ATM for cover. And if any of you haven't pulled that one, I congratulate you for having learned Rule Number Four.

For those who like casino action, stop it. You can't win. You can't win!! That's why they own the hotel and you don't. Don't build them another one. Here's a good drill. As you enter the facility, stop and watch the next twenty people coming out, and count how many look happy. It's one in twenty on a good day.

What's all this got to do with Notre Dame? Let's just call it post-graduate work in finance. It's not about making genius bets, because there aren't any. It's about not making bad ones, like: "If I lose these this four hundred, I'm going home". If that's your mindset, just give them the money and save yourself the suffering.

I'm sure I'm not alone in having broken these rules. Fortunately, less than last year and less than the year before. Hope you'll get an earlier start. See you on the first tee.

CHAPTER SIXTEEN
HALEY'S RETURN

Ohio State '32. Clements to Webber. Scoring the last seven so UCLA's eighty-eight did not become eighty-nine. Any time Joe Montana stepped on the field. Notre Dame is known for comebacks, especially the one on the front of the library.

One of her finest is a Phoenix freestyler. In '92 the team bus crashed, so did her back, so severely part was replaced with steel. First prognosis-she would not walk again. Prognosis rejected. Second prognosis- she would not swim again. Prognosis rejected. Third prognosis-she would not compete for Notre Dame again. Prognosis rejected. Sure had a problem listening to her doctors, didn't she?

When it came to prognoses, Haley Scott was a relay of rejection. For personal glory? For a book, even a movie? These thing happened because swimmers come and go, but teammates last forever, whatever the field- family, friends, or freestyle, a principle taught by Tim Welsh and Dennis Stark, coaches whose influence lasts long after graduation.

CHAPTER SEVENTEEN
A GRAVE DEVELOPMENT

Commencement - May 19, 1974, I shake hands with Ed Cronin and the Quiet Man who says: *"It's your leg on the relay now Joe."* Had to throw in that responsibility thing, didn't he? Don't you just hate coaches sometimes? My degree got me a job instantly, I started work the next Tuesday at Graver Tank & Manufacturing in East Chicago, Indiana, not in accounting but in labor at $4.75 an hour, about a Titleist by today's standards.

First day, first assignment, foreman Don Baigent: *"Son, sweep line 1."* I couldn't see the end of line 1. Second day, second assignment, same foreman: *"Son, sweep line 2."* I couldn't see the end of that one either. Ever push a broom with gusto for eight consecutive hours? In two weeks, I had the guns of Hulk Hogan. Moved up to grinding welds down on top of tank cars. Then I moved on, doing the same thing, only inside of tank cars, then a welder, a man of sparks, smoke, and sweat, at $6.10 an hours. Good lord, almost $250.00 per week, more than Gates made then. Weekends, doubles galore, would have worked triples. Burned rod (welded) and fabricated (made) seven hundred fifty-four sills (the bottom connectors) of tank cars. Four out the door a day, or so was I, so I hit for the cycle with regularity.

Friday's after work, it was Ralph's - pizza, pool, enough boilermakers to fill Ross-Ade, cash your check, and try not to leave it all there. I was not universally successful, but soon this green twenty-two year old became a different shade of tinhorn.

The factory walls were corrugated steel panels, so the winters were extremely cold. To combat it, each of us had a personal heating system all the way from Kentucky, a half pint of Jim Beam, a pint when temperatures fell below zero. What's that you say? What about OSHA? What about workplace rules? Well, this was 1974, and there were about as many rules as there were in the knife fight in Butch Cassidy and the Sundance Kid.

I also underwent an immediate change of name, as in *"having fun today, College Boy?"* and *"get me some weld rod, College Boy"* and the hands-down favorite *"you don't look so smart to me, College Boy."* Undaunted, I developed a standard response. I stole the "Go" from "Go Irish" and followed it with a *verb* and *yourself.*

It didn't take long to realize that this was not a 3-month summer stint at Inland Steel or Flexicore Construction, but a life sentence unless commuted. I decided to try the LSAT hat trick. I fooled those bastards in New Jersey this time, got a preparation book and studied, and my sentence was reduced to 15 months.

While I had the formal education, Warren Williams, Willie Williams, John Straub, Ellis Battle, and Raul Perez were the real teachers. They taught me they weren't stupid, they taught me they weren't coarse, and above all, they taught me they had the courage to serve the life sentence I did not - each a better man than I.

May I someday have the guts of the guys at Graver.

CHAPTER EIGHTEEEN
NOTRE DAME OUR FATHERS
NOTRE DAME OUR MOTHERS
NOTRE DAME OUR BROTHERS

Mostly an unused term, "Father". Did you ever ask: "Hit me some fly balls father?" or "When does the game start, father?" You knew he only went to work because he had to, instead of playing ping-pong with you. I bet your dad was as pee-od as mine was when you beat him for the first time.

Papal infallibility, the ex cathedra thing? Maybe. Paternal infallibility, for a young son or daughter? Absolutely. In politics, religion, and most importantly, the plays we should call when Lou and Ara weren't God, but held a higher position. Hard to grow out of, too. The first time I saw my dad lose a trial, I perfected the appeal in ten minutes.

Working with, I mean for your dad, is a unique and wonderful experience, but not without challenging moments. For my first three-day federal court jury trial, I was prepared for three years. When I examined my first witness from the podium before judge and jury, I felt a tap on my shoulder. I turned around, and nose to nose was Dad, who whispered: "Do you know how to refresh recollection?" A thousand points of sweat oozed from my forehead as I whispered: "I think you should sit down". My preferred response would have screamed, "You're blankety, blankety right I know how to refresh recollection, and in case I don't, I have my idiot notes right here". We worked together much better the rest of the trial; he even told me I made a good closing argument. To me, that was like I wrote the Gettysburg Address.

I learned so much from him, especially an arsenal of Western Pennsylvania lingo. Like the time I was daydreaming while raking leaves and heard, "Don't just stand there with your teeth in your mouth!" There was his description of frigid temperatures: "It's colder than a well-digger's ass in January", countered by his favorite hot weather theme: "It's hotter than a ten dollar whore on Saturday night".

Then there was his final statement of frustration: "I can't help you" and the ultimate argument concluder: "You are completely entitled to your wrong opinion". Don't think I ever won one. Glad I didn't, too. That infallibility thing holds on, doesn't it?

Our Mom and Dad left us kids very, very wealthy, and in a single document, the original bill from the William Penn Hotel in Pittsburgh, October 19-22, 1945, where they met after my Dad returned from the Philippines. Four days, valet charges, restaurant charges - total bill - $17.13. They decided not to return as clerks for Penzoil, but head to Notre Dame, a boyhood dream made a reality by the G.I. bill.

I had dedicated a separate chapter called, "Notre Dame, Our Mothers", but as usual, they declined the notoriety. Just like 'em, isn't it? In our house, Mom eventually cooked for two lawyers, a Masters Degree, and two undergraduates. My Dad was the Diocesan attorney, so we called dinner the

Cannon Law Lecture Circuit. Arguments to the right of her, argument to the left of her, arguments in front of her. Mom just smiled and watched, smarter than us all combined. Oil City High's 1936 salutatorian. Her grandson was Bishop Noll's 2006 salutatorian. Me? Call it a generation skipping transfer.

Intellectually, Mom could have wiped the floor with all of us. Instead, she just wiped the floor after giving it a going over with an old scrub brush and weathered bar of Fels Naptha soap. She opened a brand new one the first and only time I uttered a bad word in her presence. Fifty years later, the distinctive taste of Fels Naptha lingers. I hope it never leaves.

We're big on Mothers at Notre Dame, aren't we?

Mark O'Connor came into this world like gangbusters on February 2, 1950, three months ahead of schedule, and overlooking a basic skill – breathing. It took the sacrament of baptism to kickstart Mark's life administered by a young priest they would later name buildings after. But at that moment neither knew the other was the stuff of legends, when Father Ted drank some water, broke his fast, and was unable to say Mass for the only time in his priestly career.

How about that? Right at birth Mark busts up Hesburgh's perfect game. No wonder they didn't let him into Notre Dame.

Forty-nine years later I took our youngest Bill O'Connor to the Notre Dame – Louisiana State football game, a few days after Uncle Mark's surgery. We parked in Joyce South and set up a traditional tailgate. Now just so you know I am telling the whole and unembellished truth, I can tell you precisely that Bill had a sandwich, some snacks, and a couple cans of soda pop, while his dad had a sandwich and a few Budweisers.

Now this was a big, big game, a major bowl bid on the line, one of those games where electricity was surging through the parking lots long before kickoff, so when we wrapped up our tailgate, I was just about screaming when I said: "Billy, what will it be, where do you want to go, the Bookstore, the Library, the ACC ?" Then our youngest Bill O'Connor shot back in an unnerving split second: "Dad, let's go to the Grotto and light a candle for Uncle Mark." Of course, we followed that directive.

For those of you unfamiliar with the geography, the Grotto is about three miles north of a hospital in South Bend where some seventy – five years earlier a young Notre Dame senior lay dying, and when his coach came to visit, he said: "Rock, when the team's up against it and the breaks are beating the boys, tell them to go out and win just one for the Gipper. I don't know where I'll be then Rock, but I'll know about it, and I'll be happy".

Legends like George Gipp never diminish, they only grow in stature, and are joined by others. So the next time you're in church, or some other holy place, especially if you're at the Grotto at Notre Dame, take the advice and direction of an eight-year-old boy and go out and light just one candle for his Uncle Mark. We think we know where he is now, and he knows about this, and he's happy. For like Mark, we know that this event was not so much the loss of a son, a brother, a father and a friend, as the lasting and eternal union of a son with his mother, and with his older sister, and younger brother.

Terry O' Connor was as wild and reckless as roller derby on nickel beer night, and lived the most exciting twenty-six years of the twentieth century. At our traditional race day barbecue on Memorial Day Sunday of 1975, my father pulled me aside and said: "Here's $500. drive to Indianapolis, go to the city jail, get Terry out, and bring him home, he took a poke at a state trooper a few hours ago." When I hesitated, he didn't:"Shut up and get going, you'll have children of your own someday."

I cussed Terry every inch of I – 65 from Hammond to Indianapolis, where it looked like the city jail was more crowded than the Speedway. As usual, Terry was not exactly overcome with remorse: "Hey, it wasn't all my fault. I was drunk, and I'll be twenty-one in four more years." I guess that's why they call it: "The Greatest Spectacle in Sport."

Don't be misled. Terry even abandoned eternity to help others: "Guys, let me tell you about Terry O'Connor, Bishop Noll class of 1972. On a hot August Sunday in 1980, Mark, Terry, and I and some other guys were out on Lake Michigan on a boat. By the way, do you know the definition of 'boat ' on a hot August Sunday? Anything that floats that holds a whole lot of beer. When we ran out, we headed for shore and Lefty's Coho Landing, a watery dive."

While I was shooting pool in the corner, Terry approached me red-faced, with a trickle of blood from the corner of his mouth, and shouted: "C'mon, you and I are gonna fight these three guys !" I said: "Wait a minute ! Wait a minute ! Wait 'til I grab another pool cue !

At some time in the future some of you will find yourself on a boat on a hot August Sunday, or at a cookout, or tailgate, or wedding reception, or Friday after work. Always remember -The snap count is two-The snap count is two From here on out, if you ever have two units of an alchoholic beverage, the game is over, you don't drive. Go home with a friend, go home with a stranger, crawl, walk, take a cab, call a limo, but do not drive. You may not be perfect, but you will be better off than those people who don't know the snap count.

"On February, 1981, Uncle Terry forgot the snap count. Later I received this phone call: "You better go home, Terry was killed in a car accident early this morning." When that happens guys, there's no probation, no community service, no restricted licenses, nosecond chances. There is only death, and a trail of broken-hearted parents and friends.Remember, let God call your number and don't ever call your own."

A final point and we'll bring it up on two. It wasn't me who spoke to you today, it was Terry. He's here and just borrowed my voice. Look behind Sean and you will find him with Uncle Mark. It's easy to tell them apart. Uncle Terry's the one holding the pool cue. "

CHAPTER NINETEEN
LED BY TED AND NED

Joyce and Hesburgh - Hesburgh and Joyce. They were better then Hope and Crosby, Martin and Lewis, Holtz and the Option, even O'Connor and Cronin. How can you describe a priest who speaks thirteen languages? I don't know, I didn't know there were that many.

They ran Notre Dame for thirty-five years, taking us from goodness to greatness, building buildings, knowledge, values, and character. Like Hooker and Gondroff , they've kept our con, and no one knows just how they did it. Maybe it's one of those things we don't need to know, or maybe it is one of those mysteries of our faith.

Here's the best way to understand: remember the night Austin Carr got sixty-one in '71 at Ohio U? Without Jackie Meehan dishing off, Austin would have had six, not sixty-one. While Carr and Meehan connected that night in Ohio, Hesburgh and Joyce did it for thirty-five years, the scorer and the assist man, and even built the ACC in which Meehan, Carr, Hawk, Geek, Schu, and the Iceman played, breaking ground and streaks.

In '73, they brought the university's foremost initiative: gender justice. Of course, Father Ted was not confined to campus, but led national and international initiatives. He was smart enough to be appointed to the United States Commission on Civil Rights, and smart enough to be fired from it by Nixon.

Father Ted counseled presidents and popes by the score, his presence and influence covered the globe, and he never missed a beat at home. Ninety four years old and hasn't missed a beat; I wish I knew what vitamins the guy takes.

Like many university presidents, sometimes Father Ted felt like Rodney Dangerfield: "It ain't easy being me", because football coaches are not the only ones who get second guessed by alumni. This often occurs in letters to Notre Dame Magazine, but some of the toughest critics are not content with traditional expressions of discontent.

In the Spring of '71, the senior class elected William Kuntzler, Senior Class Fellow. Then I heard that unmistakable crash of a typewriter slammed on our dining room table, even though it happened seventy-six miles west of Zahm. My father created a seven page treatise describing the flaws of Notre Dame and its president, demanding that Father Ted relocate to Elba. No small distribution either, as copies were sent to every alumni organization in the U.S.. When copies reached Zahm Hall, I almost went for the Elba suggestion myself. Fortunately, our priest was forgiving. My mother was not.

There will always be controversial visits and visitors, but the supreme test of university will was given in 1971 when Tai Grace Atkinson spoke at Grace Hall and described the Blessed Virgin Mary as "a whore" and God as "her pimp". I guess that made us all "johns". There were no barriers for entry into the Notre Dame marketplace of ideas, where value was entrusted to our judgment, not to exclusion, censorship, or alumni review. The overriding policy was expression without prohibition. Ideas were not excluded, they would eventually find us anyway, and we were left to use our judgment. This was just one of the reasons Ted and Ned were so respected, teaching that better ideas will prevail without vain efforts to prohibit disagreeable ones.

Whether its Tai Grace Atkinson in 1971 or a body parts' play in 2007, controversy will find us, thankfully so. Notre Dame should continue to follow the leadership of Ted and Ned and exclude exclusion.

So much for the analytical soapbox. If you hadn't noticed, these two priests were pretty regular guys for bureaucrats, could converse at their ease and yours, went fishing for months at a time, and made time for everyone, a humanity captured in ""Father Knows Best"...

ODE TO AN EMERITUS

He came from Syracuse, New York,
and westward to South Bend
His intellectual acumen, is known to be high end
He's worked long for Our Lady; he's guided by her goals
And he's got a hankerin' for her Son,
that Guy Who saved our souls
He's counseled popes and paupers, and football coaches, too
And 'til this day he's baffled, by the lisp of our Coach Lou
He loves Digger, Dan, and Ara, and our professors, too
He loves them 'cause they lead the way, for all our students, true

Now Lord don't come a callin', stay upstairs for the day
We want Ted for 200 years, your Mom says it's okay
And when that time expires, we'll want 200 more
Lord, let us keep our Father Ted, for now and ever more

It's in ballad form now, and will be out soon?

May we love others as much as we were led by Ted and Ned

CHAPTER TWENTY
MEN IN BLACK

Of course, there were men in black other than Ted and Ned who provided direction and leadership. We found them in our dorms, we found them in campus ministry, they served in administration, and they were everywhere as chaplains. Hard to pick a favorite, isn't it?

It was Father Tallarida and Father Bill Matthews in Zahm. One weekend, I was delusional enough to think that something physical might happen, so I sought Father Bill's advice who said: "*You're taking this far too seriously, it's not a serious sin, maybe not a sin at all*". Still my personal priest, that Father Bill.

Father Griffin was next door at Stanford. His masses were S.R. O. and he even wrote a column for the Observer, "Letters from an Angry God". I've never liked that angry adjective preceding God, long been a New Testament guy fond of the compassionate and understanding adjectives. Sure hope I'm right.

Father Jim Richle was a shoe man in Detroit, turned cigar man at the Dome. Wished I'd picked up some of his other habits, too. Great guy - great, great guy.

Our first team chaplain was Father Robert Lockner a/k/a "Hollywood Bob". Had designer sunglasses before they made them. Great guy, too, but a little eccentric, like the following exchange that occurred at our post-meet meal in Olean, New York:

Larry: *"Father, there's these small round beans in my salad, I think their chi-chi beans."*
Father Bob (in lecturing tone): *"No Larry, they're girandos".*
Larry: *"Father, I don't like them very much, would you like to eat my girandos?"*

Larry is still admired by the team, the waitresses, the busboys, the cashier, our bus driver, even Father Bob, too. Told you he's a great guy.

So many, many wonderful men in black, too many to remember. I'm sure all of you have special ones who remain a powerful influence.

May they lead us where they are supposed to.

CHAPTER TWENTY-ONE
THE LAST ALTRUIST

An altruist is a person unselfishly devoted to the welfare of others. Anyone come to mind 74? Anyone we know? Maybe on the steps of the North dining hall? Someone holding a plastic milk bottle, asking for change to feed the hungry? It was harder to refuse Al Sondej than Hoss Cartwright. I kept waiting for him to say: "Aw shucks, little missy, let's go for a coke at the Huddle" or "Dadburnit Joe, can't you leave St. Mary's for five minutes, we've got chores to do."

After graduation, Al stayed true to the hungry, then became a saint, an altruist rescuing others from a burning building. Someday, hopefully a long way off, you will find yourself in new and beautiful surroundings. Then you will see the gates of heaven in the distance, throngs of angels, thousands outside. Don't be nervous or afraid, walk towards them with confidence, even smile, for when you get close, a lone angel will approach, and will shake your hand, and give you a big hug and say: "Welcome to heaven, I'm Al Sondej, let me take you inside."

When Al entered heaven, he closed the gate: "Attention, attention everyone" bellowed the big blonde: "Before we settle down into eternal bliss there's one more job to do, one last job. There's one burning building left, it's far south of here, and it's been on fire for a long, long time. There are lots of people inside, and I'm going down to get them, their boss, too. I'm going to bring them all back and end conflict once and for all. Excuse my language Lord but there's going to be a darn different result in this building. The keys to the gates of hell are at my feet. Who will pick them up and go with me?

The heavens roared and rumbled with the rush to Al Sondej. Saints and angels fought for first in line, but Father Ted and Lou and Ara arrived first with their teams. They came with the Tucson kids, along with the Quiet Man and the Y guys, now without supervision. When all heaven was ready to follow, the coaches picked their starters. Al first picked the Holy Spirit since he can cover three guys. For distraction, he had Digger wear one of his suits from 73, and for camouflage he had Father Riehle blow smoke into Hell, in greater volume than ever before

Lou and Ara prepared the game plan and Our Blessed Mother put in the Heave on the Eve, a play that worked well in darkness. Nathan Brittles left retirement to lead the assault on Hell, and said: "Who is our point, who will go first and enter the gates of hell alone?" Then, instead of boots and saddles, it was a donkey and sandals, as the Virgin rode slowly forward:

"Stay a distance Nathan, I'll find them and let you know when it's safe."Then Christ intervened: "You can't let her go down there Nathan, there's hostiles down there.""Shut up, Son" His Mother replied: "I'm giving the orders today."

The troop descended – half a league, half a league, half a league downward, until they approached the gates of the abyss, when they spotted the Virgin and a lone guard in Trojan armor. They hugged, and Mary returned to the troop. Christ again intervened: "Mother, why did you hug Hell's guard ?" "Son, that man has suffered more than anyone in Hell's history. That's Pete Carroll, and there are no mirrors in hell."

Once inside, the troop found hellunoccupied. Christ came forward and explained: "You all made it to heaven sooner or later. I wouldn't be perfect if you didn't, would I ? The hell thing? Never cared for it much, although it's proven effective with Catholcs."

And so it came to pass that Al Sondej, University of Notre Dame, class of 74, joined hell with heaven in eternal harmony, without telling Pete Carroll there are no mirrors in heaven, either.

I love happy endings, don't you?

CHAPTER TWENTY-TWO
THE MIRACLE OF THE ARTURO FUENTE

Lourdes, Fatima. Arturo Fuente? On Saturday- November 6, 2010 I arrived at my office and pulled up Notre Dame's website and an article by Shane Steinberg, a roommate of Declan Sullivan, in which he described last spring's Bookstore Basketball Tournament when Declan pulled a cigar from his shorts and played with a lit torpedo.

I am thankful for God's blessings, especially the cigar store a block away from my office. I instinctively bought a box to send to Shane and his friends, but when I left the store I noticed the nice weather. Two hours later I entered Fisher Hall and observed a single student in the lobby. I approached him and asked, "Can you help me? I'm looking for Shane Steinberg". The response, "That's me". After a speechless moment, we had a brief conversation and delivery was made. Mission accomplished.

I made three stops between the cigar store and Fisher Hall, and would not have seen Shane had I sneezed. Skeptics may refer to my father's classic argument concluder: "You are completely entitled to your wrong opinion".

I hope these events bring some small amount of comfort to Mr. & Mrs. Sullivan, whose son is always a presence, and never a memory. May God be with them until they meet again.

CHAPTER TWENTY-THREE
FEAR STRIKES OUT

You know there's only one thing worse than a young athlete that's stuck on himself, and that's an old athlete that's stuck on himself. I have been Hammond Mayor Tom McDermott Jr.'s Corporation Counsel for eight years, and was his father's attorney for nine. Both have done great things for Hammond, in their own unique style. Tom Jr. has a work ethic that would choke a horse; Tom Sr. has a three handicap and will never die of stress.

I was fired in 2000, but by someone else. Almost made it twice last November at Tom Jr's fundraiser. Five or six of us were gathered late in the evening, and the mayor waxed eloquent about his high school wrestling career, then turned to me, and I said: 'If its all the same to you mayor, I don't even talk to high school athletics.' I got outsmarted by a smarter smartass when the mayor replied:' I've got an important job for you, first thing in the morning, report to the police firing range, they'll be expecting you.' At least Mayor Tom and I have one thing in common, we are married to women smarter than we are.

I waited a long time for music ability to surface, like forty-five years, at Lauer's Bar in Calumet City the Friday of Lewinski scandal. I think the idea must have come from Bombay nowhere when I turned to my friend Joe and said 'Mony, Mony, Joe, it's Mony Mony.' Joe was not impressed, so I got even in my first book. By the way, if you need a fearless trial lawyer, Joe Stalmack and David Jensen are two of the best. David fashions himself the intellectual type, with only an occasional lapse into stuffiness. Been known to happen in my profession. I've tried major cases with Joe, or I should say I've watched Joe try them. He married someone smarter too.

Where was I? Oh yeah, then I got to work in the office and wrote the immortal 'Ballad of Bubba'. Mike Golden told me to fax the lyrics to Bill Porter, who told me they were playing Green Dolphin that Wednesday: 'Get there at 8:15 and we'll run through it.' The place was huge, and it didn't help when Bill arrived at 9:15 and said: 'No time to rehearse, we'll just go up there and bang it out.' I started looking for the exits, but I was all in, and then we did it. We did it. People even danced and fear struck out. The 'Ballad for Life' followed, then 'Martyrs of Manhattan', then 'Tucson Way' (our orchestra's favorite). Now we've done thirty. No commercial success yet, except for the September 11th Museum's posting of Martyrs of Manhattan on its website*. Our vocalist, Janice Borla, was incredible.

What does this have to do with Notre Dame? We just finished a new album titled 'Father Knows Best', a tribute to Notre Dame's revered President Emeritus. With six original songs of Notre Dame and the help of Tim and Ryan O'Neill, we've got a chance. Maybe we'll even play for Notre Dame. Another happy ending.

May I be as kind and generous as the people in this chapter.

* registry.national911memorial.org/ (Select "O")

EPILOGUE

To the people who endure through the principles they live, Mother Knows Best was written by them, not me. I am proud to be a mere hod carrier of their character, leadership, commitment, and self-sacrifice.

My leg on the relay* is over. Now it's yours.

Joe O'Connor
University of Notre Dame
Class of 1974

* Don't you love the picture on the back cover?

Made in the USA
Lexington, KY
18 April 2012